T0146697

HANDBOOK OF ESSENTIALS THAT EVERY HIGH SCHOOLER NEEDS TO KNOW

ABOUT FINANCE AND MUCH MORE!

SUNJAY LETCHUMAN

authorHOUSE®

AuthorHouse™
1663 Liberty Drive
Bloomington, IN 47403
www.authorhouse.com
Phone: 1 (800) 839-8640

Published by AuthorHouse 09/13/2017

ISBN: 978-1-5246-8807-3 (sc)
ISBN: 978-1-5246-8805-9 (hc)
ISBN: 978-1-5246-8806-6 (e)

Library of Congress Control Number: 2017905681

Print information available on the last page.

Contents

Chapter 1

Introduction/Author's Note

"Financial freedom is available to those who learn about it and work for it."-Robert Kiyosaki

The concepts in this book are in your best interest and if you take them to heart, they will help you succeed in life. All this information is simply my understanding of this world backed up by evidence from professionals and studies. Even if you did not do very well in high school, or are not doing well now, you could still very easily become more financially successful and live a happier life than the person who went to a very prestigious university because you will learn many tricks and tips to becoming a financial genius. I am just a high school junior, so why am I, of all people, writing a book about finance relating to high school students? My parents have taught me a lot about finance from the basics to some of the intricacies, but I know that a lot of parents might not be able to or have the time to teach their children useful financial skills. That's when I realized that there should be a mandatory class in high school about basic finance and how it relates to living. As an adult, if you don't understand the basics of finance, you can get into lots of trouble. After I realized that the majority of schools in the United States do not have a class about basic finance, I wrote this book. The purpose of this book is not to help you become rich (even though it will help) or to get into a good college, but instead to help you live a financially happy life. After high school, this world really does just let you go, so if you don't know this stuff, you are destined to learn the hard way: by trial and error. While you are young, it is important to establish the right framework for future financial success, and this handbook will help you establish that framework. Okay, now I think you get the point: this is important knowledge and information! Just remember, it costs you nothing to follow this advice.

What is Addiction?

"When you can stop, you don't want to, and when you want to stop, you can't"-Luke Davies

The lowest of all lows is addiction. In the coming chapters, I will be talking about activities that closely relate to addiction, so it's important to understand what it means and what it causes. Unfortunately, I have observed students who were on a straight path to success, but before they could get there, their path diverted to a road filled with health and financial agony because of an addiction. The definition of addiction is the condition of being tied to a particular substance, thing, or activity. Not all addictions are harmful; an addiction is only harmful if it impedes one's everyday activities in a negative way. For example, imagine being in an important meeting with your coworkers. Decisions need to be made, and they need to be made fast. But you're a smoker. Instead of thinking of new ways for your company to increase revenue, what are you thinking about? You're thinking about when you will be able to smoke your next cigarette. It is 'the urge' which classifies addiction; the overwhelming urge to smoke a cigarette and forget about the meeting is addiction. Addiction is a difficult battle to fight because it sucks victims in and never lets them out without lots of pain. The best way to avoid this disease is by not falling into its trap.

Chapter 2

Gambling

"Gambling is a disease of barbarians superficially civilized." –Dean Inge

G ambling is not an investment for the future. It's an investment in casino owners. Let's say after you get a job, you start to bring in an annual income of $50,000. When you're creating a budget for yourself, you decide you want to spend $500 a year on gambling, which includes scratch tickets, betting, casinos, etc. In your head, you might think it's just a measly $500, but that is 1% of your total annual income! The bad part about spending this money is that you're spending it on something completely futile; it is simply throwing money into trash cans that are collected by wealthy businessmen who own the casino or other platform.

In gambling, there's always the shrewd player and the dumb player, and you have a choice. Be the shrewd player or even better, the one that does not deal with gambling at all. For example, Organization A decides to have a small lottery for anyone to enter and this is how it works: anyone can buy a ticket for only $1. This ticket has a random combination of five numbers ranging from zero to nine. The organization is going to randomly generate five numbers after all the tickets are sold, and the holder of the ticket with the five numbers generated, in the same order, wins $5,000! You might be amazed at the fact that it is possible to pay $1 for a ticket and get $5,000 back. Although this is true, you are still the dumb player. The shrewd player, Organization A, knows exactly what they're up to. With the way they set this lottery up, there are 10^5 or 100,000 different combinations of the five numbers ranging from zero to nine, so with all the tickets sold, they made $100,000. After they pay whoever won the quite insignificant $5,000, they are left with a guaranteed collection of $95,000. Organization A wins! The moral of this story is that there is always a shrewd player and a dumb player in gambling, so when you think you are going to gamble, remember you do not want to be the dumb player.

"Hey, buddy, can you lend me $10? If I have a little more money to gamble on the table, I'm sure my luck will change." First off, your buddy asking you this should go ahead and say "have" instead of "lend" because you're not getting your money back. This is a very realistic request from a gambling addict, and if you ever get asked this question, always say **NO**! Gambling is an addiction and even the wealthy businessmen, the "shrewd ones," realize this. This is why on every casino or lottery advertisement, whether it's in a newspaper or on a billboard, there is a question in small print, which states, "Gambling problem? Call 1-800—" These numbers are simply referral services; they will refer you to counselors, addiction groups, and other groups that help stop your addiction.

All addictions lead to problems with family so a gambling addiction is no exception. Gambling addicts almost always run out of money, and their solution to this problem is to steal or cheat. For example, Bob is a gambling addict, and he runs out of money. Bob starts to use all the savings that he and his wife had for themselves and their children.

Sooner or later, Bob's wife realizes what Bob has done to his family and decides to take her kids and leave him. Now, Bob is single, has a horrible reputation, has made his kids angry and depressed, and has made his ex-wife's life very difficult. But why? Bob could avoid this distress if he just didn't gamble, right? YES! Gambling is not a joking matter; casinos today have made their interiors and exteriors look appealing and have done everything they can to make you feel like a king or queen, but all they really want is your money. The men and women who own those magnificent looking casinos and boats know exactly what they are doing, but they need people who are ignorant and addicted to gambling in order to stay in business. Don't give them your money!

One very prominent subject on the topic of gambling is parents giving kids scratch tickets. Would you give your kid a scratch ticket for a birthday present or a Christmas present? No way, right? You wouldn't want to get your kid into gambling early.... Well, think about it. If it were okay to give your kids scratch tickets, then it would be legal, but it's not. Scratch tickets give you a rush of suspense and exhilaration, but this is not good; this suspense and exhilaration is what has sucked millions of dollars out of people. If you give your kid a scratch ticket for whatever reason, it is only harming him/her. You are giving your kid an exhilarating feeling of suspense, which he/she will want again, so when adulthood comes around, he/she will be more likely to gamble.

Chapter 3

Smoking

"It is easier to prevent bad habits than to break them."-Benjamin Franklin

Money drives most of the world. So you might ask, "What's another money sucker?" Smoking. And this is the legal stuff like cigarettes, tobacco, etc. Tobacco is legal, so it is okay to smoke, right? The one-word quick answer is... **"No!"** It destroys your body and ultimately disables and kills you. Disability, or even death, results in loss of income, unhappiness, and pain and suffering for those who depend on you.

Don't learn the hard way like Whoopi Goldberg or Jon Stewart; just don't start. Many have talked about the struggles of fighting the craving for nicotine. After you're addicted, it's very difficult to quit. There are so many better places to put your money than in the hands of cigarette companies. For example, let's say you live in New York City where cigarettes can cost up to $14 a pack. Would you rather smoke one pack of cigarettes every day for the whole year, or would you rather take a vacation anywhere in the world with a budget of

$5,110? I would sure be going on that vacation! In New York, if you smoke a pack a day, at the end of the year, you would have just blown $5,110. This is not to mention all the risks your body will be taking like having a much higher chance of getting lung cancer, having a heart attack, or having a stroke. So would you rather have a happy body and a fun-filled vacation to anywhere in the world? I hope your answer is yes!

"Just try this cigarette, man. You can't be one of us if you don't try this." First off, if you are ever in a situation where you are being asked that question, just say "**No!**" and leave. They are not the type of people you want to be around. You want to become successful, rich, and live a very happy life. If you succumb to these smokers' persuasion, this poor decision impacts the rest of your life. But why would a smoker ask this question in the first place? Do smokers feel insecure with their disgusting habit, so they try to get more people addicted so that they will feel more secure and accepted? Well, smokers do have a much higher chance of experiencing anxiety, depression, and feelings of insecurity. So even if the smoker thought getting another person addicted is cool, the smoker was really just having feelings of insecurity. If the $5,110 in the example I gave earlier wasn't convincing enough, this $5,110 is only a fraction of the real financial costs. Let's say Dan has been a lifetime smoker. Yes, he is spending his $5,110 every year, but the medical costs are much greater than a few thousand. Dan has probably had to go to the doctor several times a year for treatments of colds, bronchitis, pneumonia, and chronic obstructive pulmonary disease, just to name a few. These doctor visits cost a lot of time and money, and Dan probably has to take off work, which is even more money. The stinky breath, yellow teeth, sickly cough, and wrinkled skin do not elevate his social status either.

As the years go along filled with stress, financial problems, and health problems, Dan has stressed his lungs to the limit; he needs a lung transplant.

Because of all the intricacies and complications of this surgery, the cost of it is over half a million dollars! If you thought you could go on a lavish vacation with $5,110, then think about what you could do with over half a million. The ethical factor of giving a smoker a lung transplant is another factor; if you are born with a healthy set of lungs, you should keep them like that and not destroy them.

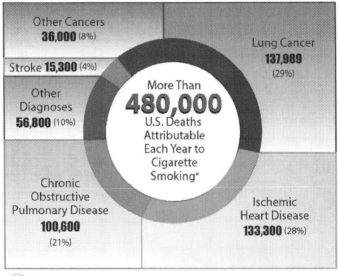

This pie chart from the CDC shows you what smoking will ultimately cause. Do you want to be part of the 480,000 people who die from smoking each year? It's your choice.

Just like gambling, smoking is a serious addiction, and the addiction usually starts early. According to the Center for Disease Control and Prevention, about

20% of high school students in the United States use tobacco products. That's crazy! Most of these kids don't have a stable source of income, yet they are participating in a costly, detrimental activity. These kids are on the highway leading straight to lifelong financial hardship. Why would they do something so stupid? The important point to remember is to learn from others' mistakes and not make them yourself. Avoiding tobacco is extremely easy; there are no legal, religious, financial, health, moral, or ethical reasons to smoke. You have the choice. Just say "**No!**" It doesn't cost you anything.

Chapter 4

Illicit Drugs

"Sometimes a parent grieves for the loss
of a child that is still alive."-Tigress Luv

The quote above is true: if you become a slave to illicit drugs, you are lost. If someone uses illegal drugs, he/she is at the lowest of lows. If someone has to smoke marijuana to "have fun," he/she is not having fun. Illicit drugs are so dangerous and just flat-out scary because so many bad things can happen to you mentally and physically.

"It's just going to be for one night. I just want to try it. I'm not going to get addicted." Please never let those words come out of your mouth because if they do, the rest of your life will basically revolve around the drug. Illicit drugs are illegal for a reason. When you consume a psychoactive drug like marijuana or methamphetamine, the drug stimulates the reward system in your brain, even though you have not actually accomplished anything worthy of reward. All the euphoric feelings obtained are from artificial sources. It all starts from the first try whether it's in middle school, high school, college, or later. That one try can decide your future. Your life will be like running a marathon and half-way there, an earthquake occurs which divides the ground, and you're not able to finish the race. If you just try it, you may become addicted, and your unique future will be destroyed.

All the millions and millions of dollars the government spends every year towards controlling illicit drug use is astonishing. Save yourself from having to go through all the rehab activities like the 12-step program or joining groups like Narcotics Anonymous or Drug Addicts Anonymous; just don't start in the first place. Illicit drugs cost drug users about 100 billion dollars a year, but that's not even close to what it costs taxpayers. It costs taxpayers more than 193 billion dollars annually due to health care costs, criminal justice costs, loss of productivity, and other expenses.

Why is it that most of the illicit drug users in the United States first try a drug when he/she is a teenager? Is it because that is his/her definition of being cool? Does he/she think that is the only way to fit in? There is no definite answer to these questions, but one of the main problems in teenagers who use illicit drugs is naivety. The teenager might have read on the Internet or heard from an uneducated friend that using drugs makes you feel cool and happy, but the teenager is too naïve to know the long-term dangers and effects. Even if the teenager does know of these dangers, he/she probably believes that such terrible things will never happen to his/her own body.

The first "try" the teenager gets from the dealer or "friend" would probably be free because the dealer knows that after the teenager is addicted, the teenager will keep coming back for more and more. The dealer will keep demanding more money as the teenager becomes more and more dependent on the drug. The teenager might steal money from his/her parents to buy more drugs to fulfill his/her craving; the overall fact is that the teenager will do whatever it takes to get the drug. The teenager becomes a servant to the drug. Also, one very important fact here is that an indicted drug dealer and the drug user are severely punished by federal law, so it's not like the user lives a horrible life and the dealer lives a happy, wealthy life; they both live a life filled with fear, insecurity, and depression. Just like I said for smoking, I'm going to say it for illicit drug use. Avoiding illicit drugs is extremely easy; there is no good reason to use them. You have the choice. Just say **"No"** because it doesn't cost you anything.

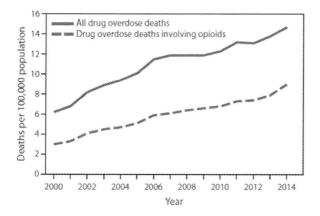

This line graph from the CDC shows the number of deaths from illicit drug overdoses. It is just so sad to see that these two lines continue to go up. Don't let yourself be a slave to illicit drugs and contribute to this upward trend!

Chapter 5

Alcohol

"Alcohol is not the answer; it just makes
you forget the question."-Anonymous

Something that is socially acceptable yet detrimental to your health and your wallet is alcohol. The quote above is a humorous way of sending the message: "Do not drink!" It is true that when you are drunk, you can forget many things and not know what you are doing. Alcohol is a dangerous drug. Almost 90% of Americans drink alcohol, yet America is one of the most progressive countries in the world, so alcohol can't be that bad, right? Well, alcohol definitely does not do you any good, and because the majority of all Americans drink, it is hard to find people who strongly disagree with it. I strongly discourage alcohol. Because of the high level of social acceptance, alcohol has become a serious and widespread problem.

Let me bring Dan back for another example. Let's say Dan is a 40-year-old teacher who makes $50,000 a year. He doesn't smoke or gamble, but he does drink alcohol. He started drinking alcohol when he was in high school, so he has depended on it for a long time. Dan is unsatisfied with the amount of money he has left after subtracting all his expenses; he's trying to figure out what else he can cut down so that his savings will increase. Hopefully, Dan takes away the alcohol! Dan has a couple drinks a week with meals, which adds up to $1,000 a year on different alcoholic beverages. That's a lot of money that Dan could be cutting down. The only reason he isn't cutting it down is he is subconsciously addicted to it and needs it. Just like I mentioned when talking about smoking, the real expense here is not the $1,000 a year to fulfill his addiction; it is the medical expenses from the huge toll his body takes from the drinking. After all the years that Dan has been drinking, he gets diagnosed with cirrhosis of the liver and chronic pancreatitis. Although it would be an extreme case to be diagnosed with both, the chances of these two conditions developing are greatly increased for people who drink alcohol regularly. Alcohol is toxic to your cells and your liver tries to immediately detoxify it the moment you consume some in an effort to save your health, but your liver can only do so much.

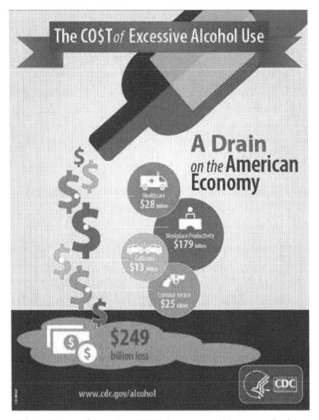

This picture from the CDC shows you how much the US economy is hurt due to excessive alcohol use every year. I've given you some of the numbers for the costs of alcohol for one person, but many hidden costs add up and affect the country as a whole.

Today, alcohol has become easily accessible. In the United States, if you are on a cruise, in a restaurant, at a store, or wherever, alcohol is most likely available nearby. Due to alcohol's widespread availability, the number of underage drinkers has greatly increased. The average age for a male to have his first drink is

11 and for females, it is 13. That is way too early to subject their growing bodies and brains to the toxic effects of alcohol. Their first drink is almost always from wanting to experiment. But why would you want to experiment with something that is toxic to your cells and doesn't give you any benefits?

I have observed teenagers who drink a lot before they go to a party or while they are at a party so that they can get "wasted." Blacking out is just scary, and anything can happen. You are unconscious, you don't really remember anything, and anyone can do whatever they want to you. Also, after a teenager starts to drink, usually he/she gets addicted, and to fulfill that addiction, the teenager needs to consume regular doses of alcohol.

Because teenagers cannot legally buy alcohol, you might ask, "How do most teenagers get alcohol?" Interestingly, teenagers get most of their alcohol from their parents. Because the majority of adults in the United States drink, their homes usually have a good supply of alcoholic beverages and many have a section or bar built to store and serve alcohol. Teenagers generally steal the alcohol that is in their homes, and because lots of parents have so many things going on in their lives, they don't notice the missing alcohol. This is not only extremely detrimental to the teen's health, but it is also teaching the teen how to swindle his/her parents and lie to them about it. If the parents of a teen do not drink, then the chance of the teen drinking is much lower than if the teen's parents drink.

Numerous websites, talks, ads, etc. advertise how drunk driving is dangerous and has caused thousands of accidents and deaths. Although this is true, an accident caused by drunk driving is the end result. The important factor to look at is the cause of these accidents and deaths. The starting cause of all drunk driving is the alcohol. A lot of people will say that you should not drink before you drive, which implies that you can drink if you are not going to drive afterwards. What we should encourage is that drinking shouldn't occur in the first place.

All of these problems and horrible situations I have talked about start with alcohol. You should learn from others' mistakes; learn the easy way. You don't want to have a family member or a close friend pass away from alcoholism or an alcohol-related accident to realize that you shouldn't drink; that's the hard way. Unfortunately, many people have had to learn the hard way before making the decision not to drink like Donald Trump who lost an older brother to alcoholism. Before you choose to drink, think about how it can hurt you. Your life is worth much more than the brief euphoric buzz that you experience from alcohol. There are so many other ways to have fun! If you go to a party, don't go drunk, go conscious. At the party, have sparkling, non-alcoholic grape juice instead of wine. Drinking the grape juice is not going to stop you from dancing, talking, and having a blast. You won't feel left out; you will feel alive, and you will remember it. So go out there and have fun—just do it without alcohol!

This information sheet from the CDC is so heartbreaking because it talks about Fetal Alcohol Spectrum Disorders (FASD). Fetal Alcohol Syndrome affects babies whose mothers drank a significant amount of alcohol during pregnancy. When a pregnant mother drinks alcohol, she is not only destroying her life but also the life of her child. Be smart; do not drink alcohol.

Chapter 6

Tattoos and Body Piercings

"Why don't I have any tattoos? It's the same reason why you don't have any bumper stickers on your Ferrari!"-Anonymous

In today's society, some people look at tattoos as beautiful body art, and although this might be true to some, in the world of the wealthy, visible tattoos are generally frowned upon. Think about it: how many wealthy people display tattoos?

Before getting into all the details, let me give you an example. There's a man named John and a man named Ben. John and Ben just got out of college with a degree in finance. Both of them are trying to join a well-established financial company to become a financial adviser. Coincidentally, they both stumble upon the same financial company. There is only one spot available, so they have to go through an interview process and other activities to see who is the better candidate for the job. They are both feeling confident, but John has a disadvantage. One night in college, John got drunk with a bunch of friends at a party. He was only 19 at the time and couldn't think straight because of the alcohol. All his friends and he decided to go to the nearest tattoo parlor because they thought that tattoos were for cool and strong people who could stand the pain. John, not knowing exactly what he was doing, chose to get a neck tattoo depicting the sun. His friends cheered him on while he was getting it, so he felt really good. Little did he know, those moments were going to cost him a lot later. Now, he is in a competition with Ben to get a job as a financial adviser at a well-established investment firm. Ben was an astute student in college and knew that what he did then would affect him later. Ben didn't participate in any risky activities like drinking and never got a tattoo. John and Ben have the same credentials and are extremely smart. However, when John goes into the interview, the first thing the board of directors notices is his tattoo. Although the sun is not a bad image, it is still ink on human skin. John impresses the directors with his knowledge and skills, but at the end of the interview, the directors know that it would not be preferable to hire someone with a visible tattoo because it looks bad in front of clients. Clients are the number one priority, so the business's greatest concern is pleasing the customer. After John finishes, Ben walks in. Ben looks natural and shows off all his skills and knowledge. The directors are impressed and hire Ben because he not only has great credentials but also doesn't have a visible tattoo (no tattoo at all!) Both of them were qualified and impressed the directors, but because John had a visible tattoo, he was not offered the competitive job. John definitely regrets his decision to get a tattoo, but it's too late.

That was a long example to say **"No!"** to getting a tattoo, especially not a visible one. Your skin is beautiful, so why destroy it by putting permanent ink on it? Most of us hate it when we get a little sharpie or marker on our clothes. We try to get rid of it with water or clothing whitener, but these are just clothes; you can get new clothes. You can't get your original skin back if you get a tattoo; it's permanent. Strictly talking about finance, tattoos themselves are quite inexpensive compared to the real cost; one relatively small tattoo generally does not exceed $500. Going back to John, let's say that John realizes his mistake and wants to fix it. He figures out that he can go to a dermatologist and get laser tattoo removal surgery. He is hopeful until he finds out that it costs $500 for one session of tattoo removal, and there are 5 sessions! The cost of the sessions alone is $2,500, not to mention the medical expenses like pain-reducing medicines. The sad part is that even after all these sessions, it is unlikely that the tattoo will be completely gone; it will most likely just be faded.

So why all this trouble for something that's only going to hurt you? One of the only ways a tattoo could help you is if you wanted to become a tattoo artist. It is imperative that you understand that tattoos do not help you become financially successful; they only impede your path to success.

Tattoos are only one of the numerous ways to destroy your skin. Another way is body piercings. Body piercings are similar to tattoos in ways like visibility as it relates to getting a job. Body piercings are unnatural and do not benefit you. Leave your body the way it was meant to be. There's nothing wrong with being natural.

Chapter 7

Eating Out

"Do not save what is left after spending, but spend what is left after saving."-Warren Buffett

O ccasionally, it's so nice to go out to eat. You don't have to cook, do the dishes, or plan and shop. The food usually comes on a nice plate served by a waiter, and your outing can feel special. But what happens when someone starts to eat out frequently? Well, then, there is a problem. The bills can add up fast.

College students and young adults usually focus so much on earning money that saving money is forgotten. Eating out may become a routine instead of being considered time out to relax or celebrate. Eating out is great but should not become a routine. To show you how the bill adds up, let me give you an example.

Let's say there is a 35-year-old woman named Sarah. Sarah works as a nurse from 8:00-5:00, 5 days a week. She makes $60,000 a year working at a hospital, which supports her, her husband, and their three kids. At work, she is always so busy, so when lunch time comes around, she just quickly goes down to eat at the hospital deli. At the deli, she spends $11 on every meal. Then, after she gets home from work, she is very tired, but she has to feed her whole family. Her husband and she just decide that instead of going grocery shopping for ingredients needed to make a meal, they should just swing by a restaurant and pick up some food. At the restaurant, the bill comes out to be $60 for the five of them, which they quickly pay without giving it much thought. Sarah's family as a whole goes out to eat 3 times a week; this is not including Sarah going to eat at the hospital's deli 5 times a week. The total adds up to about $11,280 a year; that's 19% of Sarah's income! Now, of course, food is essential, so the family should not stop eating to get rid of this expense. However, they should do the following instead. They should plan meals for a week and use some weekend time to shop for ingredients to cook at home. Many meals can be prepared without much cooking experience, and they are relatively inexpensive compared to a restaurant meal. On top of this, deli food from a grocery store is cheaper, not to mention that no tip is needed. So let's say Sarah took my advice. She started making lunch at home, which altogether only costs $3, and she would bring it to her office. For dinner, her family only went out to eat once a week, which still costs $60. With this plan, her family is now only spending $3,600! They save $7,680! Of course this situation is probably not the case for many families, but it shows that cutting down on the frequency of eating out can drastically increase your savings, and the food is usually more healthful. Even something as simple as going to the supermarket to buy a 10-pack of bottled water is so much cheaper than going by a convenient store every day to buy a bottle of water. Little things like that will save you so much money.

Speaking of eating healthy, the cost of eating out too much is only half of the problem; the other half is eating unhealthy foods. If you eat out and the food you are eating is unhealthy, long term problems develop. With over one-third of the adults in the US being obese, the number of obesity related diseases is skyrocketing. One of the main causes of obesity is fast food. Fast food might be cheap, but it's still not as cheap as cooking at home. Fast food seems convenient to grab and eat quickly and go on with life; however, life starts to slow down as one gets more obese. It's completely fine to go to fast food restaurants once in a while, but when it comes to a point where you're swinging by one every morning to pick up breakfast, there's a problem. By going to a fast food restaurant, you're just paying for the convenience all at the expense of your health and savings for your future.

For example, if a meal at a fast food restaurant costs $6, the same homemade meal made with ingredients from a supermarket would only cost $3. But just like other activities I've talked about, the real costs are the health costs. Fast food is usually filled with saturated oil and is high in calories, which contribute to obesity. Let's say John is morbidly obese and has diabetes. He spends about $8,000 a year treating his diabetes. Also, John cannot work as much as a lean person because of his physical condition and the time he takes off work to visit doctors for various other health problems related to his obesity. This loss of productivity just adds to the 20.8 billion dollars lost every year in the US because of human productivity loss. Eating healthier overall saves your wallet and saves your life.

If you are a high school student, you should start taking an effort today! In the morning, you should pack your own lunch; don't ask your parents to go to a fast food restaurant. If your parents frequently go to a fast food restaurant, it will become a habit for you to eat that kind of food later in life. For lunch, pack something healthy and fast; for example, put together a sandwich with chicken, lettuce, and tomatoes, then throw it into a sandwich bag. Doing this will train you to be a better saver later. You don't want to be Sarah or John in the examples I gave; you want to be healthy and financially clever!

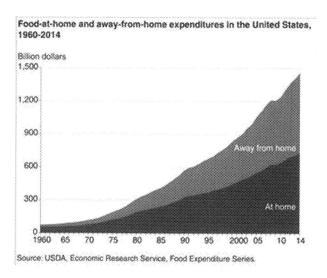

Food-at-home and away-from-home expenditures in the United States, 1960-2014

Source: USDA, Economic Research Service, Food Expenditure Series.

This graph from the USDA clearly shows how eating out costs much more than eating at home.

Chapter 8

Building your Wealth

"If you don't build your dream, someone will hire you to help build theirs."-Tony Gaskins

I've shared my knowledge on how to save your money, but now let me tell you how to earn money. Wealth is never ending, and there are three ways to earn wealth. The first way is to work for someone, which I call a Level One job. This is the most rudimentary, but it is essential. You might have a job right now, and you're probably working for someone. But why is it the most rudimentary? Usually your first job is working for someone; you learn the ins and outs of having a job and a boss. The most important thing to know about this level is that it's the lowest; you don't want to stay at this level for the rest of your life.

The quote at the beginning of this chapter represents what really happens in this world. Many people want to build their dream, but they need others to help. It is great to work for someone and help build their dream, but when doing this, you need to learn how they are doing what they do and see how you can then build your own dream in the future. Let's say you work for Corporation A as a manager. Even though you probably won't be getting the big bucks, you should still learn as much as you can and strive to be the best. Act like you own the whole business, within your restrictions of course, to simulate owning your own company. When you work for a large company like Corporation A, it is the best time to make mistakes and learn from them! It's okay to build someone's wealth while learning, but try to reach for bigger dreams. It is very possible to become significantly richer than the majority of people doing a Level One job, but becoming wealthy is a lot easier after moving from Level One to Level Two.

So what's Level Two? You are in Level Two if you earn money by working for yourself. There is a lot to understand about risk and reward at this level. When you work for yourself, you are investing everything into yourself. To explain all of this, let me give you a couple of examples.

Let's take Bob as an example. Bob has had a rough life; he lost his job, and he's struggling to make a living. Bob decides that he wants to go all out with his life by starting a business with everything he has left. Of course, this business cannot be extravagant because he does not have much, but he has enough to scratch up a little shop selling hot dogs in the middle of Manhattan. Bob is working for himself. All the profits and losses come to him and most actions that occur in his business are a result of his decisions. If the Manhattan hot-dog-market is doing well, Bob will happily earn lots of money, and he doesn't have to work for anyone. Unlike working for someone, if Bob makes a mistake, he is the only one affected. No one is there for Bob to learn from or make mistakes. This is why it might have been a better idea for Bob to start off working for a larger hot dog vender business in Manhattan, to learn the tricks of the trade, then move on to his own business. So what about risk and reward? Whenever you work for yourself, it generally goes: the more risk you take, the more reward you can expect to get. Bob's reward for his little hot dog stand has no limit, but his biggest risk is losing the $300 or so to get the stand going.

Now that we've established a rudimentary way of working for yourself, let's take another example that brings on more risk and more reward. For this example, John is the owner of his own financial advising company. He has built this company from scratch and owns 100% of the equity. He has twenty employees and manages 100 million dollars in customers' assets. Before John started his own company, he worked for a much larger financial advising company. He worked extremely hard and made sure he understood the ins and outs of the business before even thinking about starting his own. Now, he is here with his well-respected company. His risk is much higher than Bob's, but because his business is quite stable, his reward is larger than the risk. This is a great example of how working for yourself is so much better than working for someone, but it is very important to understand the risks and benefits of both.

So now we get to Level Three of ways to earn money. This is one of the most important parts in this whole book and definitely the most important way to earn money. Level Three is reached when your money works for you. Another way to put it is investing.

You and everyone else invest; you just might not call it that. When you go volunteer somewhere, you are investing your time for a greater cause. By investing your time, something is gaining or being helped. Similarly, when you invest your money in a company, that company is being helped. Many books talk about investing extensively, but I am going to give you step-by-step directions on how to get started. Many people don't realize that your money will work for you, and it will create more money that will also work for you. This process of money-growing is exponential. Many types of investments exist, and this topic can get complicated, but you don't have to know too much to do it right. Bob, the hot-dog-stand man, invested in his stand hoping that he would be able to sell enough hot dogs to get a return. This is almost exactly how the stock market works. When you invest in a publicly traded company like Apple, Google, Microsoft, etc., you are giving the company money in the hopes that the company will use that money effectively and give you more money back as a sort of interest. A stock is a share of a company, so when you buy a stock, you are buying part of a company. All these companies on the stock market are saying, "Buy some of me! Give me money; I promise I'll use your money well and pay you back more than you gave me!" In the case you do buy a part of a company and that company does better after you have invested, you receive money in proportion to how much you gave them. The more shares of a company you buy, the more money you can expect to gain or lose. Let me give an example to help.

Let's say that Albert is a 19-year-old college student with a part-time fast food job. He doesn't make much but saves every penny he can. Albert chooses to invest money into stocks. He chooses to invest in Company Z because it is a nice, stable company, which he thinks is going to go up in the months to come. He gives Company Z 1,000 of his hard-earned dollars. It turns out that he bought exactly one percent of Company Z, which means the whole company is worth $100,000. Now, he has 1% and is hoping the company goes up in value. After a month, Company Z's value is $110,000. It has grown 10%! Because Albert owns 1% of this new $110,000, he now has $1,100. However, this also works in reverse. If the company goes down by 10%, Albert loses 10% of his investment. Basically, when the company does well, Albert earns money and vice versa.

You can invest your money in thousands of publicly traded companies or stocks. When you invest, you are hoping that money is used to make more money. But what's the risk? Risk is the reason why only about half of Americans have any money in the stock market. The other half are scared everything will be lost. Even though losing everything in the stock market is possible, there are ways to invest that almost eliminate the risk of losing everything.

All iPhones have a Stocks app, which contains various letters and percent signs next to each group of letters. These letters are called ticker symbols, and they represent companies. The percent signs represent how much the company as a whole is going up or down in that day. Also, the first three rows probably went like this: DOW J, NASDAQ, and S&P 500, respectively. These are not individual companies; instead, they are something called funds. A fund is a pool of individual stocks. For example, the DOW J, or Dow Jones Industrial Average, is like a country with thirty states. Each one of these states is a stock like Johnson and Johnson, Microsoft, etc. This country has thirty states under its belt, and the success of this country directly correlates to how each of the states does. If the states, or stocks, are doing really well and producing lots of money, the country or fund as a whole does well. Also, if 10 of the states or stocks don't do very well but the other 20 do very well, the country or index fund overall still goes up that day. This is the reason why funds are not as risky as individual stocks.

If you have to transport 100 eggs from Point A to Point B using a basket, you don't want to put all 100 eggs in one basket on your first trip from Point A to Point B. You want to take multiple trips or multiple baskets just in case you drop some! Similarly, you don't want to put all your money into one company; you want to put it into a fund so that even if a couple of companies in the fund go down, the fund will still go up overall.

Numerous types of funds exist, but the most common fund is a stock mutual fund. Just as I have described before, a mutual fund is a pool of stocks, and mutual funds are generally less risky compared to individual stocks. A good conservative percent to look at as a return on a mutual fund is 8% each year. This just means that you will average an 8% return on your investment every year. Because I am not an expert in this field, I am only going to talk about my own experience with mutual funds. I invest with a company called Vanguard, which is just one of the numerous investment companies. I am not advertising for Vanguard in any way; I am just using an example that I am most familiar with. I invest in a mutual fund called Vanguard Target Retirement 2060 Fund. This fund was created for investors that want to take their money out in 2060. Remember how I talked about not putting all your eggs in one basket? Well, this is an example of that. About 90% of all money invested in this fund goes into individual stocks—both domestic and international—and the other 10% goes into another type of investment called bonds. This ensures that even if some international stocks and bonds go down but the other domestic stocks go up, I will still earn money that day. But I'm only 17, so you might be asking, "Why are you starting so early?" You should start investing now because of the power of time; a given amount of money grows over time, which is called compounding. The power of time is the reason why I say that Level 3 of making money should be integrated throughout Levels One and Two. To demonstrate the power of time, let me give you an example.

At age 15, Bill chooses to start investing. He knows that his money will grow much more if he starts investing early. He has saved all the money he has ever earned from birthdays to allowances, and the total is $3,000. Bill, being a wise teenager, chooses to invest in a low-risk mutual fund that will give him a steady return in the long run. On the other hand, Jimmy is a 30-year-old real estate agent who felt too cool to invest when he was younger. After talking to some friends and family, he decides to start investing. Because Jimmy has a moderate-income, he invests $10,000 into a low-risk mutual fund. Remember that 8% I mentioned earlier? Well, let's say that both Bill and Jimmy take out their money at age 65 when they retire. You would think that at an average of 8% every year, Jimmy would have more for retirement. NO! They actually both end up with about $164,000 even though Jimmy originally invested over triple what Bill invested. It's all because of the power of time, so start early!

Now that you know you should invest early, let me give you the steps to what you need to do using Vanguard as my example. The numerous other investment companies most likely have a very similar process to this one, so don't think this is your only option. Step one is to go to Vanguard's website. On this website, you can learn all about the company, the different types of investments, and a plethora of other information about the world of investing! Then you click "Open an Account." This will lead you to a number of questions for opening an account including questions regarding your Social Security number, bank account information, address, name, etc. I know this sounds like they are trying to rob you of your wealth, but they are not. One important thing to remember, however, is that you need to make sure you pick a trustworthy company to be investing with like a company that manages billions of investors' dollars. The process of opening an account is a little tedious because it has to deal with money, but the good thing about these large companies is that you are able to call them during business hours, and they are more than happy to answer your questions. There are five initial steps to your application: 1. Tell us about you, 2. Establish Funding, 3. Review and e-sign, 4. Sign up for Web access, and 5. Next steps.

There are some very important points that need to be noted, however. The first is that if you are younger than 18, technically you cannot invest on your own as you are considered a minor. Your parents have to make an account under their name with their bank account information. You do have your own account; it's just under your parents for legal purposes. The parent that is overseeing your account is called the custodian. They have the power to make the investments. For example, when I receive a check or earn cash worth at least $100, I give it to my parents. They go into their account and transfer, for example, $100 from their bank account to my 'minor' fund account. Then, they take the cash or check that I earned and deposit it into their bank account.

Another important point to remember is that many mutual funds have minimum investments, meaning that you can't start investing in it unless you have a minimum balance of money. Also, usually there is a minimum on the deposit, so whenever you want to put more money into your account, you have to make sure it meets the minimum. For example, the mutual fund I invest in that I mentioned earlier has a minimum initial investment of $1,000 and a minimum subsequent deposit of $100. So, first I had to save up $1,000. Thousands of websites, books, and other resources are available for more information. Just remember—invest, invest, invest!

Chapter 9

Create a Budget

"A budget is telling your money where to go instead of wondering where it went"-Dave Ramsey

N ow you know how to build your wealth, but what if you don't have any wealth to build? You might have been wondering how Bill, in my previous example, had $3,000 by the time he was 15. If you create a budget and understand where your money is going, you will start to realize you have more money than you think you do.

Telling you to create a budget is not a new concept. Thousands of resources explain the importance of creating a budget, and I am just stressing the importance of it. Let's say you are 40 years old with a stable job. You bring home $60,000 a year, and even though it might sound like a lot, you always end up running out of money or living paycheck to paycheck. Even though you might be striving to save money, you won't really realize where it is all going unless you write it down! You have to get a piece of paper and at the top, write how much you make every year or every month. Then, you need to subtract every expense you have.

Label each expense so that you know what it is. After subtracting, you will know what is left for you to save or hopefully invest. But after subtracting expenses, if your number is negative, then there is a real problem. Usually, many little expenses are overlooked, but they add up. For example, if you have a magazine subscription that charges $10 a month, you might not think that is a lot, but on top of all the other subscriptions and entertainment activities, the total adds up. Also, remember all the money suckers I discussed at the beginning of this book? If you can avoid those, you are already above the majority of people. Make a cushion for yourself and your family just in case there is an emergency. Don't cut too close. Creating a budget is critical so that you can see where all your money is going. You don't want to land up wondering, "Did all the money just disappear?" You want to find places to save so that you can invest, and you don't want to be living paycheck to paycheck, so start making a budget!

Chapter 10

Don't Keep up with the Joneses

"Rich people stay rich by living like
they're broke. Broke people stay broke
by living like they're rich."-Unknown

It is amazing how one of the easiest ways to become rich is to act like you're broke. "Don't keep up with the Joneses" is a phrase that means you should focus on your own financial status, and don't try to show off more than you have. If your neighbor is the Jones family and they have a huge house, an extremely expensive car, and other luxurious toys, you don't have to match that. You know your financial status better than anyone else; you know what you can afford and what is unreasonable. What you don't know is the Jones's financial status. For all you know, the family could be in extreme debt, and if you try to keep up with them, you will be in extreme debt, too.

You do not want to be in debt. Debt is red, negative, bad. You want to be green, positive, good. The only problem is that debt is easy to get into if you make the wrong choices. If you are in the middle class, there is no reason for you to act as if you are in the upper class. Yes, people might be impressed with a really nice house you have, but it doesn't last very long, so don't go take a huge loan out just to buy a house that would impress others. Nowadays, it is so easy for someone to get a loan from a bank or another company, but it is getting increasingly harder to pay it back. Also, a very popular way of buying items these days is with a credit card. This is fine if you have enough money to pay off the credit card bill each month, but it's not so fine if you're spending more each month than you make. Credit card companies charge around 16% interest on your credit card debt every year! Credit card debt is a serious matter. Many people have killed themselves over all their debt, which is why the US allows you to file for bankruptcy if you need to. This is not a very desirable process, so don't go down that path.

Something very important to remember is that debt is okay if it is absolutely necessary. If you just need to buy a simple house and have to borrow $100,000, that's okay if you make the process of paying it off a priority. You should be spending a significant part of your savings on paying back the debt. This means that paying off your home loan comes before cable television and other entertainment activities. Overall, you have to remember to focus on your own finances and achieve your own financial goals. Don't be persuaded by other people to spend money you don't have. Fully understanding your money and what you should do with it will lead you to financial success.

Chapter 11

Create a Legacy

"We don't live forever... Our
legacy does."-Greg Plitt

Hopefully, I have taught you many concepts of finance, and now I'm going to tell you about how your financial status can live through generations after you're deceased. As Greg Plitt said in the quote above, even though we might not physically be here anymore, our legacy could still stand. If you utilize all the financial knowledge I have given to you and become rich, you could pass that same knowledge and wealth to the generations after you. Many individuals like Bill Gates and Warren Buffett will leave a long-lasting legacy because of their successful planning and philanthropy. Both of these individuals have worked extremely hard to create their legacy. More than hard work, they are dedicated, and they do not live lavish lifestyles. These two billionaires could have so much more material wealth than they actually do, but they choose to have an impact on society as a whole by helping out and encouraging others with wealth to do the same. They learned to gain financial knowledge and live by it their whole lives while still being happy. You can do the same and leave a legacy that will be remembered for centuries. You don't want to make mistakes like Michael Jackson who was on the verge of filing for bankruptcy because of his poor financial planning and spending. You, instead, want to leave a good financial legacy. Financial stability is a gateway to happiness. Once you have achieved stability, you can enjoy life with your family, friends, and others. Hopefully, I have equipped you with the necessary knowledge to become financially stable, so go out there and create a legacy because now you have the essentials that every high schooler needs to know!

Acknowledgements

There are several people that I would like to thank for helping me make this book possible. I would first like to thank my parents, Rama and Santhi Letchuman, who taught me the bulk of the knowledge in this book. I would also like to thank Mrs. Barbara McGuire, my junior english teacher, for proofreading this book. There are many others that influenced my decision to write this book, and I am truly appreciative of all of them.

Printed in the United States
By Bookmasters